AFFORDABLE
ART DECO
GRAPHICS

Susan Warshaw Berman

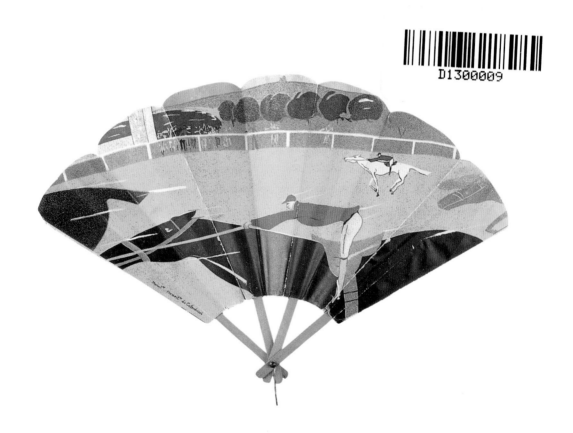

Schiffer Publishing Ltd

4880 Lower Valley Road, Atglen, PA 19310 USA

Dedication

To the memory of my Aunt Roslyn Salny,
who was an author.
To Clare Murphy, whose words of wisdom
ringing in my ears started this project.
And to Joshua and Lindsay, the lights of my life.

Designed by "Sue"
Type set in Broadway BT/Humanist521 BT

ISBN: 0-7643-1476-9
Printed in China
1 2 3 4

Authors photo: Judy Rittenhouse

Published by Schiffer Publishing Ltd.
4880 Lower Valley Road
Atglen, PA 19310
Phone: (610) 593-1777; Fax: (610) 593-2002
E-mail: Schifferbk@aol.com
Please visit our web site catalog at **www.schifferbooks.com**
We are always looking for people to write books on new and related subjects. If you have an idea for a book please contact us at the above address.

This book may be purchased from the publisher.
Include $3.95 for shipping.
Please try your bookstore first.
You may write for a free catalog.

In Europe, Schiffer books are distributed by
Bushwood Books
6 Marksbury Ave.
Kew Gardens
Surrey TW9 4JF England
Phone: 44 (0) 20 8392-8585; Fax: 44 (0) 20 8392-9876
E-mail: Bushwd@aol.com
Free postage in the U.K., Europe; air mail at cost.

Contents

Acknowledgments

I would like to thank Debbie Sullum, who started me on my flea market and antique addiction. I would also like to thank the following people who helped with my research: Dr. Henry Lehrich; Tom and Judy Dawson; Linda Bailey at the Cincinnati Museum Center; Ron Kurpiers at the Minnesota Historical Society; and Fred Wallace at the Framingham, Massachusetts Historical Society. Thanks to my friend, Judy Rittenhouse for editorial advice and support, to Myra Yellin Outwater for her sound advice, and to my husband Larry for just being there. I would also like to thank the very kind and helpful people at Schiffer Publishing, especially, Doug Congdon-Martin, Jeff Snyder, Donna Baker, and Peter and Nancy Schiffer. To Robyn Stoltzfus: thanks for the cookies.

Introduction

The *Exposition des Arts Decoratifs et Industriels Modernes* in Paris in 1925 introduced Art Deco style to the world. All the finest artists, designers, and craftspeople of France got together and displayed their best in every area of art and design. Furniture, sculpture, painting, clothing, posters, architecture, glass, graphics, and even candy box labels and packaging were some of the things on display. Many countries had exhibits showing the latest in modern design. Germany, being the enemy of France in World War I, was not invited. The United States did not participate either, because Herbert Hoover felt that we could not compete in the design arena. We did, however, send a contingent to study the art and design of the exposition and bring the ideas back home.

The beginnings of what was to be known as Art Deco, however, can be found in a variety of forces in the early 1900s. Diaghilev's "Ballets Russes," with its sets and costumes designed by Léon Bakst, brought oriental style and color to France in 1908. The opening of Tutankhamen's Tomb in Egypt in 1922 influenced artists, jewelers, and designers all over the world to use the Egyptian motif. A show of Black African art in Paris in the 1920s influenced the designers to start using African themes in their work. The Bauhaus in Germany, led by Walter Gropious and Marcel Breuer, contributed a new concept of design and style. The Dutch de Stijl movement and cubist painters like Pablo Picasso and Fernand Léger influenced a rethinking of traditional forms. Artists traveled to Mexico and the American southwest, bringing back the Aztec and Native American influences. Finally the Jazz Age in America and Hollywood all contributed to the Art Deco style.

Actually the multi-cultural style of Art Deco had many names, including Art Moderne, Streamline, and Machine Age among others. The design elements of lightning bolts, ziggurats, stepped-up designs, light rays and circles all combined to make Art Deco graphics stand out. The stylized flowers, the slim, naked women, the streamlined cars, and the use of striking geometric and curvilinear designs were recurring themes in Art Deco design, as was the use of animal motifs such as gazelles and leopards. Deco typography adopted sans serif type and saw the introduction of new typefaces such as M.F. Benton's "Broadway" and "Parisian," Eric Gill's "Sans," and W.A. Dwiggins's "Metro," to name a few. It wasn't until 1966, however, that the name "Art Deco" was used to describe the conglomeration of styles that took over the world from 1908 until 1945.

Collecting Art Deco Graphics

The search for items with Art Deco graphics has become an obsession for me. It is a look and feel that I never tire of. It takes me back to what I think was a very romantic, glamorous, and sexy time period.

The great thing about collecting Art Deco graphics, and fortunate for me, is that you don't need a lot of money to do it. The items that I have included in this book are affordable and for the most part are easily obtainable with a little searching.

Art Deco graphics are part of a large collecting area known as ephemera. The definition of ephemera according to one dictionary, is "anything having a very short life." The 2001 Merriam-Webster's online Collegiate Dictionary has added collectibles to its definition.

Among the collectible ephemera are advertising, letters, cards, theatre programs, and menus, all excellent sources for Art Deco graphics. They have a short life because, first, they are made of paper, and, second, they were originally meant to be discarded after use. That this ephemera exists at all is testament to its beauty.

Some suggestions here about buying paper.

- **First, use your nose!!** That musty and mildew odor will not come out of the paper so don't buy it if it smells.
- **Second, remember that condition is most important.** Paper should be clean, not torn or written on.
- **Third, it should be complete**. A magazine or book should have all of its pages and its covers. (Of course, when you just want it for the ads or picture, it doesn't matter as much if it is in bad condition.) If you are buying playing cards, they should be a complete deck in the original box. I have included a more detailed guide in the beginning of each chapter.

Prices depend on condition and also on where it is bought. Something bought at a yard or garage sale will cost a lot less than the same thing purchased at an antique mall or shop. Internet auction sites such as eBay have a great selection of paper and ephemera, but if someone really wants something that another bidder is interested in, you will have to pay a higher price for it. One of the best sources for buying paper and ephemera is a book and paper show, many of which are held around the country. At these you can see it, smell it, and have the widest selection.

A word about price stickers and tape. I don't understand why a person who deals in paper and ephemera would put a glue-backed sticker right on the item, but I see it all the time. I know that the stickers says "removable," but trust me, in 99% of the cases, they are not! The other nemesis is tape. The only kind of tape that does not damage paper is the Scotch tape that is called "removable" and comes in the BLUE box. You can find it at the big office supply stores. The best way to remove price stickers and tape is with a hair dryer. If you are patient, it will dry out the glue, but it doesn't always work. I have ruined many things trying to get price stickers and tape off of them.

I have divided the book in to seven different chapters, but certainly some of the categories overlap. All items in the book are from the 1920s, 1930s and early 1940s unless stated otherwise. The country of origin is given for each item. If the country is not mentioned, the item is from the United States.

Chapter 1
Greeting Cards, Playing Cards, Bridge Tallies, Place Cards, Games, and Other Ephemera

The bridge craze in America began in the late 1920s. Bridge games were the entertainment at many social events. Whether it was a luncheon, shower, birthday or holiday, bridge was played. This intense interest in bridge begat an industry of paper goods. Companies published hundreds of different bridge tallies, bridge score pads, place cards, bridge sets, and playing cards, all with vibrant, colorful Art Deco graphics.

Because there were so many of these made, great examples with terrific graphics can be found almost anywhere. Yard sales and garage sales are good places to look. They can also be found in box lots at house auctions, although they are rarely listed in the newspaper ads for the auctions so you have to go and look. Paper shows have a large selection.

Prices vary according to condition. Have they been written on? If you are buying bridge tallies, are they clean? Are they bent or torn? If it is a complete set does it have all the pads and tallies? Does the set come in the original box and what is the condition of the box? The other variables in bridge items are the publisher and the subject. It seems that the most popular tallies are the ones that have the very beautiful Art Deco ladies on them. Halloween themed items in today's market get higher prices than any of the other holidays. The variables for place cards are about the same as for bridge tallies.

Playing card prices depend on a number of factors. Is it a complete deck with the joker or jokers. Is it sealed or has it been opened? Has it been used and how worn are the cards? Are the cards in the original box and what is the condition of the box? Are they artist-signed? Is the deck rare or common? How old is the deck and who was the publisher?

The largest publisher of playing cards in the United States is the United States Playing Card Company. It was started by John Lawrence and Solomon Cohen in 1871 as the New York Consolidated Card Co. In 1881, Russell, Morgan and Co. merged with the company. It became the United States Printing Co. in 1891 and the United States Playing Card Co. in 1894.

As for publishers of bridge tallies and place cards, the Buzza Company is the most sought after. Other popular companies are the P. F. Volland Company, the Gibson Company, Rust Craft, the Henderson Line, Charles S. Clark, and Hallmark.

Rust Craft Publishers began in 1906 in a room in Kansas City. It moved to Boston in 1916 and was known for artistic books, mottoes, and greeting cards. They also had a line of bridge-related items.

In 1850, George Gibson moved his family of nine and his French-made litho press from England to Cincinnati, where the four youngest sons started the business. They did commercial engraving of checks, bonds, and stocks and they also printed labels for perfume, liquor, and drug packaging. During the Civil War, Gibson started producing stationary and prints by Currier & Ives. Even though the company had its economic ups and downs, by the 1920s it employed 1300 people and produced more than 150 million greeting cards in a year. This was also the time of the bridge craze and Gibson was producing bridge tallies, pads, and place cards that were vibrant with amazing Art Deco graphics. In 1950, Gibson celebrated its 100th anniversary and employed more than 5,000 employees. For the first 100 years, the company was known as the Gibson Art Company with the emphasis on art. In the late 1950s, it became Gibson Greeting Cards, Inc. In 1964, it was bought by C.I.T. Financial Corporation but retained the Gibson name. In 1973, it introduced the greeting card rack and shelving system that is still used by card stores today. In March 2000, Gibson was taken over by American Greetings and is no longer using the Gibson name. American Greetings moved the business to Cleveland.

The Henderson Lithographing Company started in Norwood, Massachusetts in 1856 and published a line of bridge tallies and related items along with many other paper products.

One of the most collectible publishers is the Buzza Company. It was founded in 1908 by George A. Buzza. He had the advantage of being trained as an artist, designer, printmaker, and engraver. The company was originally known as the Buzza-Rheem Company because of Buzza's partnership with a promising young artist named Royal Rheem. When Rheem died prematurely in 1909, Buzza decided that, with his artistic background, he could produce a unique greeting card. The cards that he started to make in 1910 stood out in the industry because of their vivid colors, good paper stock, and the fact that they were hand-painted. Buzza started to produce place cards in 1911, and followed with a full line of greeting card and stationary items in 1916. In 1923, Buzza moved the company to a larger facility that he named "Craftacres." A line of party and bridge related items was published there, as well as children's books and the famous Buzza Mottoes.

In 1929, Buzza retired to California, but the company stayed in Minneapolis until the early 1940s. Once in California, George Buzza decided to go into business with Ralph Cardoza, who had worked for Buzza in Minnesota. Cardoza had been president of the Charles S. Clark Greeting Card Company, New York, which was part of The Buzza Company. The new company became Buzza-Cardoza. Cardoza stayed on as president of the company until it was bought by the Gibson Art Company in the early 1950s. George Buzza, who had retired years earlier, died in 1957. Mr. Cardoza died in 1965.

George Buzza's vision of making distinctive and unusual greeting cards for the public still holds true. The Buzza Company designs stand out as some of the most beautiful Art Deco examples of their day.

I have also included games and other ephemera in this category because of the beautiful Art Deco graphics. These are easily found at flea markets and garage sales.

The following are some wonderful examples of Art Deco graphics on greeting cards and related ephemera.

Greeting card store display. $50-100.

Trade magazine. *The Greeting Card.* 1931.

Advertisement from *The Greeting Card* for Gibson Art Company stationary products.

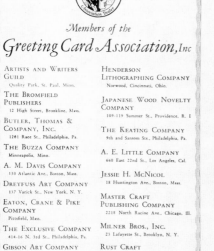

Page from *The Greeting Card*, listing the stationary companies that are on the board of the magazine. These include, Buzza, Gibson, RustCraft, and Henderson.

Five decorative Christmas cards. $4-12 each.

Three decorative get well cards. Top, 1937. $5-12 each.

Four Valentines. Top two are postcards. Bottom left, Rust Craft with real eraser. Bottom right, The Buzza Company. $5-20 each.

Three Christmas cards. Bottom left, Christmas post card. $4-15 each.

Left:
Three decorative birthday cards. Top, Keating. $5-12 each.

Right:
Four decorative Christmas cards. $4-12 each.

Three decorative New Year's cards. $5-15 each.

Two large decorative Christmas cards. $5-15 each.

Three birthday invitations. Bottom left,
P. F. Volland Company. $5-15 each.

Top left, Easter card. Bottom left, Easter card,
Hallmark. Right, Thanksgiving postcard. $5-15 each.

Left, commencement card with envelope. Right,
sympathy card with envelope. $8-20 each.

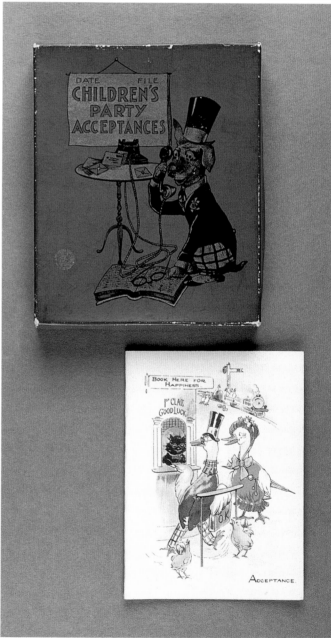

Children's birthday party acceptances. Six with
envelopes. Alexander Baird & Son. England. $40-55.

Children's party invitations. In the Little Folks box are six invitations, envelopes and acceptances. England. $40-55.

Autograph book and box. Artist: Estelle Frantz. 1930. The Reilly & Lee Company. Chicago. $30-50.

Page from autograph book. Teachers.

Page from autograph book. Dogs.

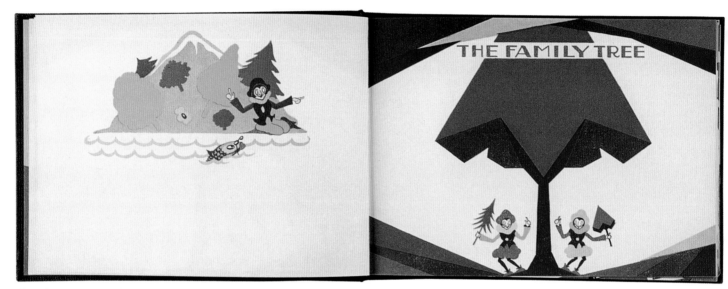

Page from autograph book. The Family Tree.

Unframed motto. The Buzza Company. $10-15.

Top, Christmas gift cards in box. Bottom, Christmas gift seals in box. P. F. Volland Company. $15-20 each.

Close-up of Christmas gift cards in box. Gibson Art Company.

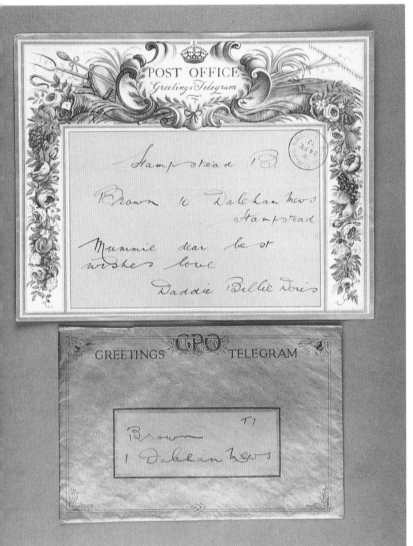

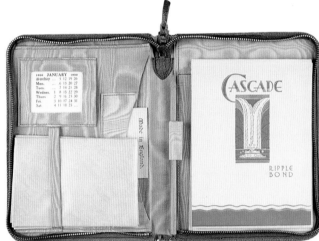

Leather stationary folder with calendar. 1936. England. $15-35.

Decorative greetings telegram with envelope. 1937. England. $15-25.

15

Decorative greetings telegram with
envelope. 1936. Western Union. $5-15.

Decorative greetings telegram with envelope.
Artist: Walsh. 1939. England. $15-25.

The 1920s and 1930s produced the most beautiful and interesting playing card backs.

Two leather bridge
cases. $35-65 each.